MASTERING THE BUSINESS OF YOUR ASSOCIATION™

No more condo commando

Jane F. Bolin, Esq.

Jane F. Bolin, Esq.

jane@PeytonBolin.com

954.316.1339

Twitter: @janefbolin

LinkedIn: https://www.linkedin.com/in/jane-bolin-17124b8

Copyright © 2017 by Jane F. Bolin, Esq.

All rights reserved. No part of this publication may be reproduced, distributed, or transmitted in any form or by any means, including photocopying, recording, or other electronic or mechanical methods, without prior written permission of the publisher, except in the case of brief quotations embodied in critical reviews and certain other noncommercial uses permitted by copyright law. For permission requests, write to the publisher, addressed "Attention: Permissions Coordinator" at the address below.

PeytonBolin, PL

3343 West Commercial Blvd, Suite 100

Fort Lauderdale, FL 33309

Printed in the United States of America

Table of Contents

PROLOGUE: i

Setting Your Intention

INTRODUCTION: iii

Why Great People Can Still Get Poor Results on a Community Board

CHAPTER ONE: 6

Lessons Learned

CHAPTER TWO: 12

Why Associations Need to View Themselves as a Business

CHAPTER THREE: 18

How Boards Govern Themselves When They View Themselves as a Business

CHAPTER FOUR: 28

Trusted Advisors: Who Are They and How Should You Manage and Interact with Them?

CHAPTER FIVE: 43

The Business Cycle of Associations

CHAPTER SIX: 47

Key Performance Indicators for Community Associations

CHAPTER SEVEN: 54

Getting in Action: Board Strategy and Alignment

PROLOGUE

Setting Your Intention

Before you start reading this book, take a moment to determine what you'd like to get out of it. Seems like a strange request, right? However, I'm asking you to do this because you already know the basics about being an association board member – or about community associations in general.

First, let's define what we mean when we use the word *associations* or *community associations* throughout this book. There are several types of association boards, including condominium, homeowner, mobile home park, and cooperative. They are all governed differently because they are different types of not-for-profit corporations. But for the purpose of this book, we'll use the term *association* to describe them all.

Perhaps you've had the experience of being a community association board member and thought it was challenging. Or maybe you think all associations are run poorly. Maybe you loved your experience as a board member and thought your association was well-run. They are your experiences and you're entitled to them.

More than anything, my goal in writing this book is to spark a much overdue conversation in the industry that will change the way community association boards are run and what it means to be a board member or manager. In order for you to be fully engaged in this conversation, I'm hoping you'll approach the new ideas you find here with an open mind, as a blank slate, so this book really makes a difference for you and your community. That may sound like a bold statement, but I'm committed to making a difference in the community association world and believe that once we distinguish what has been missing, the world of community associations will transform.

So if you've had a moment to think about it, what do you hope to get out of reading this book? Are you out to enrich your community? Are you looking for a new way to think about things? If so, this is the book for you. If you're not sure of your intention at this point, I invite you to try on some things I'm going to share and see how they fit before you make a decision.

Sound good?

Great! Let's get started.

Introduction

Why Great People Can Still Get Poor Results on a Community Board

As a community association attorney, I've seen firsthand that most associations and their boards aren't working as well as they should.

Why is that? How can you put together a group of intelligent, skilled people, who are typically successful in other areas of their personal lives, and get such poor results? In my experience working with community associations, I've discovered some common elements between boards that run well and boards that don't. This book presents a new perspective on community associations and what it means to be an effective, engaged board member or community association manager, and I'm excited to share it.

The Inside Scoop on Community Association Law

First things first: What makes me qualified to lead this conversation? I got my first taste of community association law when I was a clerk for a small law firm. A case came along that was the association against the developer, the management company, and the attorney. I was given the task of legal discovery – which meant I was responsible for requesting documents, ledgers, policies, procedures, and balance sheets – documents that would support our case. This gave me the opportunity to learn about Florida condominium law. The common element I uncovered as I was going through the discovery process was the poor quality of documents and information we received. Ledgers were confusing and many policies and procedures had to be recreated. I remember thinking there was an opportunity here and that this didn't have to be so hard. I got a real understanding of Community Association Management (CAM) requirements and what it took to do this well in the industry.

From there, I became a licensed CAM and asked the managing partner of that law firm to go into business with me. We started a property management company together in 2006. We set the business up and started marketing ourselves to associations. Within a short period of time, we had one client, then five clients, then 10, 20, and so on. When we sold the company in 2010 we had 26 associations as clients.

After I graduated law school, I immediately went out on my own and set up Jane F. Bolin, PA, representing associations. At the same time, I was also running the property management company. Even though they were separate entities and there was no actual conflict, I did think there was a perceived conflict of interest. I realized that where I had the opportunity to make the most impact was not in managing associations but in helping them from a legal perspective.

The Start of PeytonBolin

My entrepreneurial spirit was alive and kicking and I quickly became interested in expanding the law firm. I landed my first big hurricane damage case and reached out to find another attorney to work with me on it. This is when I met my current partner, Mauri Peyton, who was introduced to me by a mutual friend. We enjoyed working the case together and came to the realization: having a partner really works. That experience, coupled with the opportunity to represent associations, led us to the creation of a partnership and PeytonBolin was launched in June 2008.

At that time, it was Mauri, myself, and our receptionist – in a small office space with a conference room and a handful of clients. We kept growing and needing more space. We moved three times within our first office, adding more offices and blowing out walls to accommodate our expanding team. In 2014, we bought a 4200-square-foot commercial building in Fort Lauderdale, FL, that currently serves as our headquarters. PeytonBolin has grown year after year since its inception and today, we have over 25 employees managing hundreds of associations in Florida from our headquarters and satellite offices in Orlando, Tampa, and West Palm Beach.

Our firm has achieved many accomplishments, including winning the prestigious Reader's Choice Award from Florida Community Association Journal for legal services three years in a row, being selected to the Inc. 5000 list in 2015, being distinguished by SuperLawyers.com, which is part of Thomson Reuters, and being cited in media outlets such as The Wall Street Journal, NBC, Fox, and CBS. This has reinforced our commitment to making positive differences for the associations we represent and teaching board members how running an association like a business leads to success.

CHAPTER ONE

Lessons Learned

As PeytonBolin grew and we added more associations, Mauri and I started analyzing our business and having conversations about what kind of clients we wanted to work with and what clients for whom we were able to make the most difference. These conversations exposed a number of important lessons that we had learned over the course of our work with community associations:

1. **The best association clients are able to make decisions.**

    We distinguished that board members who could make decisions were not only our favorites to work with, but were also the ones we could truly make a difference with. The one common element that associations with decisive board members had was they viewed the association as a business. The lightbulb flashed on and PeytonBolin's *Mastering the Business of Your Association* education program had its genesis.

2. **There are usually two types of board members: The overly engaged and the not engaged at all.**

    You will have more engaged board members when you treat your association like a business. Board members who understand the bigger picture and their place in making better board members will succeed. Disengaged board members will eventually struggle to add value to the association and ultimately will not help it fulfill its mission. When you have a board full of non-engaged members, it's a clue to a bigger issue. (see #8)

3. **Associations need more education on how to deal with their trusted partners. Hire professionals and then let them do their job.**

    Association boards hire attorneys for their experience and then don't listen to us. We've also seen this with boards that hire property managers and then don't let the manager do their job. This behavior is detrimental to the association. Board members often don't realize the impact of not letting their trusted advisors do the job they were hired to do. Board members for companies like Coca-Cola and Apple know their role is to make decisions in the best interests of the corporation's shareholders and consider the advice of management, counsel, auditors, and other independent consultants. When community association board members view the association as a business, they understand how important it is to think and act like corporate board members and listen to their advisors.

4. **Boards have no idea what they are accountable for.**

    Most associations don't have a training or onboarding process to educate new board members on what their role is and what they are accountable for. This leads to many board members unknowingly doing things that may be contrary to statutes or their governing documents. Without proper guidance, they end up doing things "their own way," which is never best for business.

5. **Professionalism goes a long way.**

Having structure and professionalism in all board settings goes a long way. The way you treat other board members, unit owners, your trusted advisors, and your employees has a profound effect on how your board runs. Creating and following a structured process that supports your association's mission, vision, and values – a culture of professionalism – makes a big difference in the success of your association.

6. **You have to create boundaries.**

   Boards hire trusted advisors for a certain level of service and the fee associated with that service. A common side effect of a poorly run board is that it then has a different expectation, which typically involves the advisor being available 24/7. We learned to address this early on, both in our contracts and in our conversations, so we set the proper expectations for the relationship right from the beginning. For us, it was really important to be clear that our job wasn't to be a "yes person," but to do what the boards we worked with hired us to do. But it works the opposite way as well. When a board is run like a business, they'll create contracts with their advisors that detail what the advisor will and will not do, as well as the cost of any additional services. Boards that are run this way are much more desirable as clients and partners.

7. **Don't take it personally.**

   This was a tough lesson for us, and it was personal. We had worked with an association for several years and had done really great things with them. We helped them turn around their collections recovery, which had over half a million dollars in past due assessments. Then a new board came in and they didn't like the management company. Even though we were separate and distinct from the management company, they associated us with them.

Bottom line? They didn't like us.

But we couldn't accept that. So we kept meeting with them to prove how valuable we are, and showing them all the results we had produced for the previous board. We must have spent over 20 pro bono hours trying to repair that relationship. And then one day we just realized, it wasn't working; this particular board wasn't in alignment with the past board or us. We finally realized that we wouldn't be able to work together.

It was scary, but as soon as we let it go and realized it wasn't personal, that it was just business, the proverbial weight lifted and freed us up to focus on clients we were in alignment with. But the only way we were able to accomplish this was because we viewed ourselves as a business. When you view your board as a business, you're able to remove the personal agendas and vendettas that cripple many associations.

8. **If recruiting is tough, it's usually always part of a bigger issue.**

A lot of people agree to be on a board to be "nice" or out of a sense of obligation, feeling like "I live here so I should volunteer here." This doesn't sound like it would be an issue, but it is. Over time, you get a bunch of "nice" – or worse, "power hungry" – volunteers who have no idea what they are doing or, more importantly, why. Eventually, this leads to a low-quality board, which makes it tough to attract new board members. Boards that are decisive, well-structured, professional, and that view the association as a business, not as a volunteer job, will find it much easier to recruit and retain high-quality board members.

9. **Building a community means doing more than just following the statutes.**

Boards should have clearly defined roles and responsibilities that members can easily understand. An association is a not-for-profit business that is subject to specific requirements, like tax returns and corporate filings, just like any other business. All associations are governed by state and federal law. In Florida, an association is governed under Florida Statutes Chapter 718 for condos, Ch. 719 for cooperatives, and Ch. 720 for homeowners, and Ch. 617, which is the not-for-profit statute that also governs associations

Far too often I've seen boards live by the letter of the law and do just what is "required." And listen, you can do that, but I wouldn't recommend it. Remember, this is a community where people live and raise their families. If you want your community to be more engaged, you should communicate with them more. Having a monthly newsletter, a website with ongoing updates, and a way for owners to easily communicate with their board can lead to a healthier association.

Also, in your board meetings, you can decide what works for you. Yes, if you want to follow "the rules" you can limit how long a unit owner has to speak, but think about the effect that has on people. This is something I talk to board members about all the time. If you want to be able to recruit community members and get them involved, you have to give them a say in the matter.

As I've mentioned a few times, the foundation for a successful board and well-run association is viewing your association as a business. Let's go into more detail about why that is and the process for making that happen.

CHAPTER TWO

Why Associations Need to View Themselves as a Business

For starters, because they are one. Like we said earlier, your association is a not-for-profit business that is subject to specific requirements, such as tax returns and corporation filings, just like any other business. There are specific legal obligations you want to have clear regarding your association. A big difference between corporate boards and association boards is that association board positions are volunteer positions elected by popular vote. Association board members are not required to have specialized skills in one particular area of the business as they are in a corporation. Instead, members are selected based on their expertise and skill, or simply by being liked by others.

The majority of association boards today don't have a vision for their community or even big goals that they are working toward. They may have projects they are working on that change year-to-year depending on the priorities of the individuals on the board. Now, one might say that the vision of any association is probably something like this: *provide quality services to their homeowners and protect and preserve property values.* Not a bad vision, but the path to get there will vary from community to community.

When associations view themselves as a business, board members develop and define their mission and vision so all residents and other trusted advisors (which we will talk more about in Chapter 5) know what they are trying to accomplish. When board members understand their mission and vision, they can develop clear pathways to their realization. This allows board members to stop the busywork and moves them toward being productive, which creates a much more fulfilling experience for everyone.

1. **Deep pockets**

   Community associations are considered deep pockets, which is a key reason that they need to view themselves as a business. Despite the fact that they may not have large budgets, they still have insurance policies; if there is a personal injury or crime takes place, it's important to have an insurance policy that truly protects the association.

   When boards realize their association is considered a deep pocket, it puts a whole different light on how seriously you take selecting and/or renewing insurance policies. Instead of renewing it because that's what the statute says, association board members realize they need to protect the association and make sure they have the right coverage and liability amounts.

   It's important for association board members to understand that when a liability occurs, the injured party will look to who has the ability to compensate, which in this case is going to be the association. If somebody slips and falls in Target, they're suing Target. Associations are in the same boat.

   If the association doesn't have the right kind of insurance, they won't be able to protect the association and, ultimately, it's members from financial exposure, such as special assessments. Many associations don't realize this because they don't think they will ever get sued. Conversely, business owners are acutely aware of the potential for getting sued and take precautions to ensure they're protected. When you view your association as a business, you recognize that you need to make good business decisions, not emotional ones, and protect the community.

2. **Take the emotion out of it**

    This idea is at the heart of PeytonBolin's *Master the Business of Your Association* education program and my biggest reason and inspiration for writing this book. People get emotional on business boards, don't get me wrong, but it's typically not tolerated. When it comes to association boards, however, it seems that emotional board members are the norm, not the exception.

    So why is it that an intelligent, well-respected professional who accomplishes amazing things in their career loses their mind when you put them on the association board? The biggest, and perhaps only, reason is that the issues being addressed affect where they live, so it seems okay that they take things personally.

    A lot of times board members aren't even conscious that the way they act in an association board meeting would never be allowed, even by them, in any other setting.

    So why is it so normal in the association setting?

    Because board members don't view the association as a business. They view it personally.

    Having outside resources, like general counsel on your team, is extremely useful because they can help present to you the facts so you can take the emotion out of it. And when you can distinguish that the difference between those two states of mind, the transformation that takes place is incredible.

3. Businesses invest in themselves

What drives communities is their desire to avoid assessments and increased HOA dues because that affects them personally. Why would I want to pay more? In fact, making sure assessments don't go up is a key motivation for many people who become a board member.

When board members view the association from this context, they miss the fact that they need to constantly make investments in the community. They miss that you have to spend money to keep your property values higher, to keep your landscaping up to date. You've got to spend money to save money, right?

When board members view the association as a business, they understand that the purpose of the association is to protect and preserve common elements and increase property values. They know that their role is to uphold that. This understanding simplifies many things and, more importantly, aligns board members to that common vision.

Let's look at an example: ABC Community has been around since the 1970s, has always been a nice community, and its board members have been vigilant about keeping things "the way they've always been." So the board is not being open to investing in upgrades because they don't wanted to incur any special assessments; it's what works for the majority of the board members personally.

Right next door, DFG Community, which was also a nice community in the 70s, has kept up with the times and made significant upgrades to the community. This community appeals to current and future residents. So guess what? Property values of DFG are significantly higher than property values of ABC because DFG board members are interested in enriching the community, as well as protecting and preserving it. They've researched how to be a more environmentally conscious community and have invested in LED lighting, South Florida friendly landscaping, and LEED certifications. This appeals to younger buyers who are willing to pay more to live in a more modern community.

Because DFG Community views itself as a business, it's natural for them to make these investments because it supports their overall vision.

The association is ultimately a not-for-profit. It's not there to generate revenue or create a profit. It's there to protect, preserve, and enhance. That's really the whole point. That's why associations have a zero tax return. Yes, they still have to file, but it's meant to be a zero tax return because it keeps them in that not-for-profit status, where they're not getting taxed on income that comes in.

When boards stop viewing their association as their own home, take the personal aspect out of it, and start viewing it as a business, the decision-making gets much easier. The board will start making decisions that may personally cost members money, but support the vision of the association, which makes good business sense.

This results in a better run board that is fulfilling and enjoyable to be part of. Board meetings become more productive and, lo and behold, decisions get made based on what makes good business sense instead of emotions and personal agendas. All of a sudden it's not so hard to recruit new board members. Instead of a culture where everyone is against something – new assessments, other's opinions and just change in general – the board is for something. A better community, a vibrant association, an inviting place to live, higher property values. The list can go on and on. So how should a board that views itself as a business govern itself?

CHAPTER THREE

How Boards Govern Themselves When They View Themselves as a Business

1. **How a nonprofit board gets formed**

    Boards are run very differently in the corporate world, which sometimes causes confusion amongst association board members. Association board members think if they have an officer title, they somehow have more power than anyone else. Association boards are what I like to call small democracies. Everyone has the same vote despite officer titles. Board members can have different responsibilities but decision-making is collective.

    Residents in a community vote to elect their board members. Most of the time, depending on the governing documents, board members will then choose the officers amongst themselves. Board members are officers, and officers are board members. Whereas in the corporate, for-profit world, a board is chosen and then the board hires the officers, who are not people on the board, to execute duties.

2. **Board documents**

    Governing documents are association documents, which include Articles of Incorporation, Bylaws, Declaration of Covenants, Conditions and Restrictions (CC&Rs), and rules and regulations. An association's governing documents serve as the foundation for how a board should govern itself from a technical perspective. These documents will cover things like how many board members there are, the role of each member, the structure of board meetings, and other important components. It's important to have clear documents that are thorough and complete. Unfortunately, many associations use a template that the developer provided them before the association was turned over as their documents. These documents may not reflect the best interests of a unit-owner-run association. They may also have been done so long ago that they are not up-to-date with the times. This is a good place to start when determining how a board should govern itself. Look at your documents and make sure they are relevant in today's world. If they aren't, consider amending them.

3. **Setting the context for being an association board member**

    I mentioned at the beginning of the book that I wanted you to set an intention for reading this book so you didn't read everything through the filter of your past experiences or preconceived notions. You may be finding that hard to do, or you may not even realize that you've been doing it because it's happening subconsciously. You are quietly agreeing/disagreeing, classifying certain things as good/bad, right/wrong, or makes sense/doesn't make sense. We all have filters that run us unless we distinguish them, which allows us to notice when we are coming from an "I already know that" context.

    This same thing happens with new board members if you don't create the context. People come onto a board thinking it works a certain way. Maybe they think it will be like the last board they were on or maybe they think boards are run like those they've seen on TV shows like *The Apprentice*. Context is everything, and it's super important to set the context for how you want board members to show up, how you want meetings to be run, and how decisions are made. The most powerful thing you can do is to make sure you set, or reinforce, the context every time you bring your board together. If you don't, your board will fall back on old ways or bring with them whatever they were dealing with prior to walking into the board meeting (e.g. their day at work).

In order to truly understand "context," I'm going to have you do an exercise, courtesy of Townsend Consulting Group (www.TownsendConsultingGroup.com), a performance coaching and professional development company we work with at PeytonBolin.

> A newspaper is better than a magazine.
>
> A seashore is a better place than a street.
>
> At first it is better to run than to walk.
>
> You may have to try several times.
>
> It takes some skill, but it is easy to learn.
>
> Even young children can enjoy it.
>
> Once successful, complications are minimal.
>
> Birds seldom get too close.
>
> Rain, however, soaks in very fast.

Too many people doing the same thing can also cause problems.

One needs lots of room.

If there are no complications it can be very peaceful.

A rock will serve as an anchor.

If things break loose from it, however, you will not get a second chance.

I suspect that the paragraph made little or no sense for you. Let's try it again, this time using the context "Kite."

Definition of Kites

A newspaper is better than a magazine.

A seashore is a better place than a street.

At first it is better to run than to walk.

You may have to try several times.

It takes some skill, but it is easy to learn.

Even young children can enjoy it.

Once successful, complications are minimal.

Birds seldom get too close.

Rain, however, soaks in very fast.

Too many people doing the same thing can also cause problems.

One needs lots of room.

> If there are no complications it can be very peaceful.
>
> A rock will serve as an anchor.
>
> If things break loose from it, however, you will not get a second chance.

Just add the context and it makes sense. This is why setting the context before every conversation is so powerful and why some conversations make no sense.

You want to set the context for how board members view their roles. You will want to say something like, "Hey, in this board, we view the association as a business, not personal. That means we don't make decisions on how they may affect us personally, but how they support the mission and vision we've set for the association which, by the way, you've already shared or created with your new board members. That means you may be FOR SOMETHING, or support something, when viewing the association as a business that you may not necessarily be for, or support, personally."

This is so powerful, and you can do it for everything. You can start each board meeting or conversation by creating the context of why you are there and what you are up to. You can get really clear about the fact that we all might have different views on how to achieve certain things and that's okay, as long as we are all coming at it from the same context. When you first read the kite exercise without the context, it was confusing, right? That's what it's like when board members start expressing their opinions based on what matters to them personally. It can be very confusing. But when you create the context, everyone can get on the same page.

So if our context is "as a board, we are here to create actions that will protect and preserve property values and enrich the community living experience for our residents," then we can be open to the fact that individual board members will have different ideas on how to get there. And that's really great. Not everything will get done based on your timeline or your terms, but if we set priorities as a business, it will likely get done. If your board is doing the right kind of planning, i.e. one-year, three-year, five-year planning, which is how a business does it, then you'll be able to say, "Maybe you won't get that playground this year, but it's on the schedule for year three," and everybody wins. One of the tools we've created for boards is an Association Meeting Planner, which helps board members break down their yearly commitment into goals and action steps that align with the overall board mission and vision. Visit PBMBA.com to download it (password: game-changer).

Creating the context for every conversation is really powerful in crisis situations too. Let's say your association needs a certification and the county is threatening to come in and shut you down (i.e. unit owners must move out) unless you get that certification within a certain time frame. That's a legitimate crisis that could cause a lot of emotion amongst board members, and you've got to deal with it. But you can deal with it much more powerfully if you've got a powerful context for it.

Instead of dealing with it from the position of how much it's going to cost, you can begin to look at what it really means to be threatened by the county because your buildings haven't been upgraded. How are we going to deal with it? Will our unit owners be able to handle the cost? Are there some creative financing options? Are there additional opportunities we can take advantage of as we are dealing with this? Are you just going to handle what needs to be done and be done with it? Or will you determine whether you can enhance the community while you are doing it? All of a sudden the conversation becomes invigorating instead a conversation about desperation.

This type of thinking will open up all types of new possibilities for your board and your association and will impact your structure and decision-making. Let's talk more about that.

4. **Power and Freedom**

   Just because something is in your board's governing documents doesn't mean you have to do it exactly that way. Everything doesn't have to be black and white. Yes, I know that initially it may make you nervous thinking that people might get to infuse interpretations, but if you are all coming at it from the same context and viewing your association as a business, you might want to consider how you can carry that through in your interaction with your residents. Don't get me wrong: having good documents in place that you can refer to is vital to the success of an association, but just because it is in your documents doesn't mean that's the *only* way to do it. There are other possibilities when you're running your board like a business.

   For instance, the documents may state that there are certain decisions that the board can make on their own without involving the residents. But when you are viewing your association as a business and are interested in creating a strong community, you may want to consider opening it up for discussion before the board votes.

5. Imagine the difference that could make

Yes, you will hear some opinions you don't agree with, but they may add value to the conversation. In our experience, they often do. And because residents feel like they are being heard and that their opinions matter, they will want to show up at board meetings. You won't just get the people that come for the free coffee and donuts or worse, who just want to complain; you will start to get residents showing up who are interested in sharing and contributing and may make great future board members. Instead of including unit owners in board meetings because you have to, you include unit owners because you've created an environment of transparency and inclusiveness. Yes, you will want to adhere to reasonable rules and regulations about the frequency, manner and duration of people's statements, but are you going to just view them as statements or are you going to be open to the possibility of what your unit owners have to say? You can create the context that you actually want to hear from your unit owners and meetings can actually include some laughs and lightheartedness. This makes it much easier to create an involved community and to recruit future board members. There's a lot of power and freedom with boards that choose to do this and you will begin to develop strong leadership within your community when you do.

6. Getting the community back in communities

There are a lot of great ways to create a community in your community. When boards want to involve and engage with their unit owners, all sorts of possibilities open up. People get more involved, it's easier to recruit, the community starts to thrive, and the association vision gets realized. And then, you actually get to know the people in your community, make some friends, and have some fun.

Most people don't spend time getting to know their neighbors because everyone is so busy working, raising their families, and dealing with whatever they are dealing with. It's not hard to find ways to take the time to get to know people in the neighborhood, find out who they are, what they are up to, what their interests are. For instance, the board could create a campaign where each board member is responsible for going out and interviewing three unit owners in the neighborhood that they've never met. Board members go door to door and introduce themselves and ask them questions. "Hey, how's it really going for you? What do you think of the neighborhood? Do you have any ideas you want to share?"

I've also seen communities create newsletters and Facebook pages that help unit owners get to know each other and serve a useful purpose. Again, you have to create the context so the Facebook page doesn't become a place to lodge complaints, but instead a place where people can interact with one another: "Hey I've got this Cuisinart Deep Fryer I'm not using anymore for $10. Anybody want it?" or, "Are there any pet sitters who can watch my dog next month?"

You can create a sense of community that people really love and that enriches the community living experience.

I hope you are starting to get a clear picture of the difference it makes when community associations view themselves as a business and how boards govern themselves when this is the context they are coming from. Let's talk about how you can extend this to your trusted advisors.

CHAPTER FOUR

Trusted Advisors: Who Are They and How Should You Manage and Interact with Them?

A community association will have several trusted advisors, with the main three being:

1. Community Association Manager or CAM: This can be one person or a company that supplies a team
2. Certified Public Accountant (CPA)
3. Association Lawyer

Out of these three, your CAM is going to be your association's #1 Trusted Advisor. (Note: If you are a self-managed community association, then your attorney will be your key trusted advisor.)

Licensing requirements may differ by state, but for the most part, CAMs are licensed by the state, which means they are required to pass a test and, in order to keep their license current, must also invest in continuing education.

A community association manager can be a huge asset to a board. In an ideal world, the board is strategic, they make decisions, and they see the big picture. Then they ask the community association manager to execute it. Mostly that is not how it is when associations do not conduct themselves as a business. Let's dig a little deeper into the day to day role of a community association manager.

3 key CAM responsibilities include:

1. Building: The physical assets of the association.
2. Administrative: Administrative duties such as dealing with statutory notices, responding to clients, being the point of contact for unit owners.
3. Buffer: Being the point of contact for unit owners so board members are not.

A CAM may be responsible for all of these things, or the responsibilities can be split up where the board does certain things. A huge component of what a CAM does is to act as a buffer between the board and the residents and to help direct the board. When boards view themselves as a business, they understand that there is a cycle to the year and that various things have to happen during different times throughout the year. We'll talk more about this in Chapter 5, but for now all you need to know is that your CAM will help direct this. There are certain filing requirements every year, e.g. financial reporting with the State, annual report filing for the Florida Division of Corporations, and tax filing, and then there are budget cycles and election cycles. Those are the big ones every year, and then there's also all the stuff that happens in between, like the day-to-day maintenance for the property, planning and scheduling long-term projects and special assessments. And then big projects that may come up like handling property damage or major reconstruction.

A CAM is like your financial portfolio manager. They manage your assets. You give your portfolio manager your money and they manage it for you. They aren't someone you hire like a secretary or assistant; they are professionals trained to manage your community assets, deal with other trusted advisors, serve as the buffer between boards and residents, and execute the strategic plan of the association and board.

In our experience, we've seen all different levels of CAMs and how boards interact with them. Many associations view their CAMs like administrators that are told what to do. That's a very different relationship than viewing your CAM as a trusted advisor who is given the freedom and space to execute on the association's mission and vision.

Some boards want more control while others want to empower their CAM to make decisions. Each CAM will have a different level of competency and that may dictate they type of management style you have with them, but I think it's important to remember that CAMs are licensed professionals. They have been trained and are held to a fiduciary duty, just like board members. They also have a wealth of information that can be of value to your association. So you can choose to have CAMs that are order-takers or you can choose to have CAMs that are more sophisticated and act like consultants. Either way, they should not be expected to be experts at everything: roofing experts, plumbing experts, irrigation experts, landscape experts, collection experts, etc. However, as a trusted advisor, the CAM should be able to bring forth vendors for these services that they've either worked with in the past or for whom they've gotten referrals. The CAM can bid out for projects or ongoing work and provide that information to the association board.

The Opportunity

In this section, I am providing action items you and your board can act on immediately to begin running your association like a business. The opportunity I am referring to here is the opportunity to run your association in such aa way that creates and amazing experience for everyone involved: board members, unit owners, and trusted advisors.

Getting clear

The number one complaint most CAMs have about boards is they don't make decisions. The number one complaint boards have about CAMs is unfulfilled expectations. The opportunity here is to get really clear on how you want your relationship with your #1 Trusted Advisor to work and what that actually looks like in reality.

Imagine if your board had a conversation about what it will look like to work together when interviewing a potential CAM? What if you were able to get really detailed around that and ask questions like:

- ☐ How quickly will you respond?
- ☐ Can I have your cell phone so I can reach you anytime?
- ☐ How do you handle litigation?
- ☐ How often do you do walkthroughs?
- ☐ Is there a specific day and time you do walkthroughs?
- ☐ How do you handle emergency situations?

It starts to sound more like an interview, right? Well, it is. And just as a business would ask a potential employee many questions and vice versa, so too should CAMs and community associations.

Some other things to note in this section are the different ways CAMs work with specifically with community associations. An onsite manager has a very different relationship than a portfolio manager. As an onsite manager, they are there day in and day out. They know the property. They know the people. They have office hours where people can come in and speak to them.

Smaller associations that don't need this level of service will usually hire a portfolio manager that provides onsite services but works with other associations as well. They devote a certain amount of hours each week to your community and simultaneously handle a number of other communities as part of their portfolio.

When working with a portfolio manager, it's important to understand what they have to offer in terms of the support of their team and how they are actually set up. Are they going to assign one key contact who acts as the community association manager? Do they have a violations department, a client services department where unit owners can call, a maintenance department? All of those things. You want to find out what teams they have, how the CAM works with those teams, and how those teams work with you as clients.

You'll also want to find out how many communities your potential CAM manages and determine how that will impact the service they can provide your community. How many hours will they dedicate to your community a week? When you're looking at the contract for a management company, the clarity there is so important. They may promise financials before every meeting, but what form do they come in and what does it include? When your association is being run like a business, you have the foresight to ask for specific things, such as a sample packet of financials and the management packet, before you meet with or hire anyone. You'll be able to determine their experience level and ask questions like:

- ☐ How long have they been managing?

- ☐ What kind of communities have they been managing similar in size?

- ☐ Have they had any complaints? (You'll want to check with the division to see information.)

- ☐ Have there been any actual complaints on their licenses? What was included?

You can also perform background checks on any potential CAMs. You can do reference checks and speak to a variety of references, and not just the good ones they're going to give you.

Now maybe you are already working with your CAM and you didn't go through a process like this. Do it now. Set up a time every year to go through what it looks like to work together and where you can improve. We suggest doing a review after the first 90 days with a new CAM and then periodically throughout the year. The guidelines for what will be included in that 90-day, quarterly and annual review should be laid out in advance so everyone is clear on what the expectations are. This leads to the next point: The Contract.

Reviewing the contract

It is important to review the contract with your CAM at least once a year. Many times, board members think they have access 24/7 to their CAM, but that's not what is in the contract. They may think that the CAM should oversee a special project that is happening on a weekend, but don't realize that is above and beyond what is in the project and should be treated like a special project.

For instance, if an association is going to have their parking lot re-paved, they may say something like, "Well, we want you to be there when they're repaving the whole time," which is well above and beyond what may be stated in the contract as "managing vendor relationships." You've got to look at it from the reality of time. If it takes three days from 8 to 5 to repave the parking lots, you're asking your CAM, who may only have X number of hours a week dedicated to your community, to be there from 8 to 5. That's more like what we would call a special project and is probably outside of the contract. Now, there are many companies that just bite the bullet and do whatever the board says because this is such a competitive space and they don't want to lose their clients. But if this is the nature of the relationship, it won't make for a very good one over time.

The problem with a lot of CAM contracts is that they don't allow for the contingencies that invariably come up, e.g. the unit that burns to the ground, the water leak that happened Saturday morning at 3am. How are you going to handle that? Most contracts don't clearly detail what it requires to handle the situations that arise. There could be a certain amount of emergency responses in the basic contract and then anything over that is charged at an hourly fee. If you are reviewing your contract with your CAM periodically, as any business would, you can determine what else needs to be detailed so all parties are clear on how the relationship works as it progresses.

One of the issues I see is that many community associations want to spend the least amount on their CAM, so they go for the cheapest price. But it's going to be challenging for your CAM to service your association the way you want if you don't allocate the resources to do so. If you are viewing your association as a business, you will choose your CAM based on what makes best business sense, not what is the cheapest.

Surveys

Another great opportunity is for CAMs to survey the board and the association periodically to learn what's working, what's not, and where the opportunity for improvement is. Boards should also ask to be reviewed by the CAM:

- ☐ How are we doing?
- ☐ What's it like to deal with us?
- ☐ Is there anything we could be doing better?
- ☐ What are you seeing with other homeowner associations that we can learn from?

You might not like what you hear, but if you are interested in fulfilling your vision and mission you need to know, right? You can also survey vendors that deal with CAMs and even a random selection of unit owners. For instance, if you just completed a project where you worked with a landscaping vendor, survey them afterwards to find out how it was to work with the CAM and community association. Or if a unit owner had an issue recently that needed attention by the CAM, send them a survey. It could even be an informal conversation. You just want to make sure you do enough surveys to get valid feedback. You will always have those unit owners that are never happy and will never give you a fair run. Surveys are a great way to get feedback that can be used to continually grow and improve the community.

Let's say an association wants to look into green technology because they want to save money. They're going to look into solar lights or digging their own well. Under a normal contract, they're dealing with utilities, etc., which is really outside the scope of a normal contract. And mostly boards, they don't want to spend more money to have the CAMs do that work, but they want it to be done, so they either do it themselves or they give the direction to the CAM. OK. They picked this company to do these things and those things and wonder why the CAM resists, when instead they could say, "Okay, this project is going to require this much time outside of the contract. We're going to pay for that." Mostly, we see associations that just expect their CAM to do that because it's "part of the utility" or "part of vendor management," but that expectation is so inappropriate.

When you're clear on the responsibilities you want your CAM or any trusted advisor to hold, you can build contracts around those expectations and be really clear on what is and is not going to be handled by your advisor, which eliminates confusion and creates a solid working relationship that can last for years.

The Buffer

I touched briefly on a key role that CAMs play around being a buffer between the board and the residents. There are quite a few ways this can play out. One of the roles is during meetings.

CAMs can actually run the meetings for the board or they can assist the board in running the meeting. When I say "run the meeting," I actually mean run through the agenda, i.e. call it to order, roll call, and control each section of the meeting and the time limits. Or the CAM could assist as the board member runs the meeting, perhaps by taking notes, meeting minutes or being the timekeeper.

When the meetings come about, the CAM will generally provide what we call a management packet, which usually includes financials, occurrences in the community, the maintenance report, the violation report. That's provided for the board prior to the meeting so the members have ample time to review and prepare so they can be responsive during the meeting. Just like board members for companies like Coca-Cola and Apple get their board packet to review well before the meeting so when they get together they are informed and prepared and respect everyone's time, so should association board members.

I think the best practice is that the board runs its own meeting. That's what it is. It's a board meeting with a management report. However, if you don't have a strong board or a board that can deal with unruly unit owners, but you've got a strong CAM, then you can put the CAM in to run the meeting.

Regardless of who runs the meeting, your CAM can be an important buffer between the board and the unit owners. Board members are unit owners, but in this context they are wearing a different hat. Your CAM can be the buffer to deal with unit owners who may be speaking too long or bringing up things that are not on the agenda. They can do this in a very professional, business-like manner that keeps the meeting from getting emotional.

So how else is a CAM a buffer? Since it's not best practice to have unit owners go knocking on the doors of board members to lodge complaints or request maintenance, CAMs can also serve as the buffer here. This is a key area where I like to counsel board members to use their CAM to create the buffer that says "I'm not available for my neighbors at any time just because I'm a board member." This goes back to creating very clear systems and processes on how these things are handled. It should be as simple as, "You have a maintenance issue. If it's not an emergency, fill out the online maintenance form on our website. If it is an emergency, call this number." Board members should not be the emergency number. That's a big thing that turns people off from being on the board. It's a volunteer position. You have your own weekend. Your weekend isn't meant to be the time where you're required to do walkthroughs of the community. If a board feels like they need to do that, then it points to them not having the right CAM.

Another area where the CAM can serve as a buffer is with other trusted advisors. The CAM can be the point of contact with your CPA and your attorney. We recommend that you always have a board member who manages these relationships as well and is copied on all correspondence. Again, it's important to lay it out in the contract. Having this type of clear communication will help ensure expectations are fulfilled. This is another way your CAM can serve as a buffer and execute on the vision that the board has laid out.

Other Trusted Advisors

As I mentioned at the beginning of this chapter, your community association manager, or CAM, is going to be your #1 Trusted Advisor unless you are a self-managed community association, in which case your attorney will likely fill that role.

Community associations typically keep their bookkeeping in house, but having a trusted CPA who does its taxes and is able to advise the association on financial management issues is key. Some associations may also need a financial advisor as one of their trusted advisors, which may be part of the CPA relationship or a completely separate relationship. If a community association has a large reserve account, your board may need financial guidance to determine whether a regular money market account, a CD or some other option is best.

As I said earlier, your CAM can be the point of contact with your trusted advisors, but it's important to have checks and balances in place. Having someone on the board who is always copied on and involved in these conversations is vital. This doesn't mean the board or the board member needs to deal with every item, but that their eye is always on it and they are determining which items can be delegated to the manager and which ones need to be handled by the board. In my experience, the association is usually more involved in managing anything to do with legal and financial advice. I see the CAM managing the landscaping relationships, irrigation relationships, painting relationships, and construction. It's like a three-prong approach, and I think the best practice for the board is to have somebody that's involved with both the CPA and the attorney.

In choosing the right attorney for your association, it's important to choose one that has specific expertise with community associations. Association law is its own niche, and just like I said about CAMs, being a valuable association attorney means providing a full range of services and being able to deal expertly with insurance, contracts, personal injury, covenant enforcement, and statutory enforcement. You want to make sure you have a firm that's in the space and not just someone who's an attorney who practices association law. I think it's important that you work with a firm who has decided this is their practice area and are experienced in working with the boards, homeowners, and other trusted advisors. Note: it's a big red flag whenever any of your trusted advisors throws other advisors under the bus. That just doesn't work. It's got to be a team approach.

I think this goes for all trusted advisors, but when choosing the right association attorney, you want to make sure they are responsive and communicate in language you can understand, that they provide actual legal guidance, break down complex matters, and offer your board multiple billing options (e.g. billable hours vs. flat fees). You want to look at their breadth and scope of experience.

We love the team approach, especially when the CAM invites our firm and the CPA to board meetings to talk about the year. Today, this is unheard of, but it's one of the things we are creating with our board strategy and alignment training. We hope this book gives CAMs the resources to lead that conversation and be powerful advisors to their boards. CAMs are often who boards look to for help finding other trusted advisors, so team approach is critical.

Empowering Your Trusted Advisors

The community association board should empower – *not* micromanage – all of their trusted advisors, especially their CAM. For instance, I hear complaints from boards that focus on documenting and managing community violations whose violation committee gets upset if the manager goes out on their own to do walkthroughs without involving the committee.

If you trust your manager, you're not micromanaging their day. They know what they are accountable for and do it. You may want to know when and how often they are doing it so you know it's being done properly, but managers should be allowed to go walk the property without committee involvement. There are ample software programs where they can take pictures and report violations to ensure the work is being done. When you run your association like a business, these responsibilities would be clearly defined in the management company's contract. If you're a self-managed community, the association may want to invest in software programs that allow committees to take pictures of violations.

You can see that the work is being done without micromanaging your CAM's daily routine. But "we'll do a walkthrough once a month" is not a clearly defined responsibility. Unclear responsibilities lead to unfulfilled expectations. The board thinks the walkthrough will be done on this day at this time, or that it would take only so long to complete, but because there is no clearly defined schedule, the CAM creates their own. Clearly defining the responsibility means you determine who will own it and how they will fulfill it. In this example, you would want to determine how your CAM performs a walkthrough, when they do it and how often, what that looks like (is it a drive-through or are they actually walking through), and how they will report those findings to the violations committee. When you get this level of clarity in your contracts and invest in the tools you need to support your trusted advisors, you eliminate unfulfilled expectations. Then it's just a clear expectation between two people or two entities. If they don't do it, they don't do it and you can deal with the impact of that.

This is much clearer and easier to deal with than, "We think you should be doing X," which is often what I hear. "We think our management company should be doing that." I say, "Well, have you guys looked at your contract?" Usually, the board says no. If they haven't looked at it, how can they be clear on what the contractual obligation is? Get clear on your expectations, lay it out in the contract, and then keep it alive by discussing it at periodic intervals throughout the year.

When associations view themselves as a business, it is enjoyable to deal with trusted advisors because expectations are clear and communication is effective and positive. You aren't basing conversations on how you feel or your emotional state. You are dealing with facts and reality and dealing powerfully with what is working and what is not. Your trusted advisors are vital to the execution of your association vision and strategy.

CHAPTER FIVE

The Business Cycle of Associations

"We are what we repeatedly do. Excellence is therefore not an act, but a habit."
- Aristotle

Just like businesses have cycles, so do community associations. Yet many association boards haven't taken the time to identify their cycle and use it to create a rhythm for how they manage their association. When we refer to "The Business Cycle of Associations," we are specifically talking about taking a look at the year in its entirety and identifying what there is to do and handle throughout the year.

These are the 5 key elements that make up most boards' annual business cycles:

1. Elections
2. Budget
3. Financial Reporting
4. Special Projects
5. Assessments

It's powerful to understand your association's business cycles and what things need to happen before, during, and after each element in the cycle in order to have a successful year. So starting with elections, getting new board members certified, having the strategy meeting for the year, coming up with the top 3-5 things the board is going to focus on for the year, and what success looks like at the end of the year. By understanding and planning for each of these things proactively, boards create a consistent rhythm on how to run the association and actually know what they are dealing with versus having things creep up on them. This creates structure and predictability, which is a good thing. Predictability leads to success.

Let's take a closer look at how this looks in action. If you have elections every November, you start talking about and planning for them in June. That can actually be put on a meeting agenda so it never gets overlooked. And I don't mean it gets put on the June meeting agenda manually – like someone has to remember – I mean it's already on there going into the year, that there are meeting agendas as part of the board packet that automatically take into consideration the association's business cycles. As you look at your business cycles, you proactively plan what needs to happen and by when, before, during and after each element.

By proactively discussing elections six months prior to them happening, you can have brainstorming conversations about how elections will be handled, who from management is dealing with it, how you'll encourage people to run and how you'll create a culture in your community where unit owners actually want to participate on the board. Instead of frantically talking about elections in September or October when you're stressed and desperate, you can create a plan and talk about them powerfully. Can you envision how much fun those conversations would be?

The same thing goes for financial reporting. When it's part of your annual business cycle, you start talking about your financial reporting needs early to make sure you've got a reliable trusted advisor to do the report. If you don't, you are able to spend time finding a new resource versus having to stick with the old one because you haven't allowed enough time to identify, interview, and select a new trusted advisor. You can also discuss and plan for more strategic conversations such as:

- ☐ Have we done a reserves study?

- ☐ Are there any building trends we want to investigate to determine if we want to factor them into our financial plan?

- ☐ What impact would those projects have on property values?

- ☐ What other things should we consider and discuss to ensure our financial planning is supporting our overall vision and mission?

By understanding and managing the business cycle of your association, you are always one step ahead of the game and can spend time being proactive (instead of reactive), which makes it a lot more effective and enjoyable to be on the board. It also sets you up for success instead of just maintaining the status quo.

Your conversations around your community association business cycles also depend on what stage your community is at. Are you brand new, have you been around forever, or are you somewhere in between? An older community should be sure they are looking at current trends so the community doesn't appear old and out of date. Things like community WiFi access, demographic shifts from retirees to families, data security concerns, and electric car charging stations should all be discussed because they will affect your goals and your budgeting. If your board isn't having these type of conversations, you will fall behind the times very quickly, which will impact your property values. If part of your mission and vision is to preserve and protect property values, which it should be, this means you aren't doing your job.

How do you know more precisely what to look at, what to measure, and what success actually means to your association? That brings us to our next chapter, where we'll discuss key performance indicators (or "KPIs") for community associations.

CHAPTER SIX

Key Performance Indicators for Community Associations

You can't manage what you don't measure. - Peter F. Drucker

A key performance indicator (KPI) is a measurable value that demonstrates how effectively an organization is achieving key business objectives. Companies use KPIs to evaluate their success at reaching targets. Effective KPIs are vital signals that help indicate if your business is functioning according to plan.

Let's break it down:

- ☐ **Key:** An important or vital aspect. It means you have to prioritize. However, it doesn't mean you can leave everything on the list and just shift the order of priorities. Everything you measure can't be considered a key metric. Start with a manageable number. We recommend you start with 3-7 KPIs.

- ☐ **Performance**: The manner in which something operates, functions, or behaves. Just like an engine's performance can be measured by more than its miles per gallon, a company's performance needs to look beyond metrics such as collecting of assessments.

- ☐ **Indicator:** A sign that gives information about and draws attention to a condition. This is usually a number, percent, or color code that quickly conveys a favorable or non-favorable status.

Some indicators are only seen from the rear view and are historical in nature, like sales, or from an association perspective, collection of dues. If you look at the number of delinquencies at the end of the month, there is nothing you can do to impact it that month. It's the number. We call these lagging indicators. Then there are predictive indicators. So in the case of delinquencies being a lagging indicator, the leading indicator might be the number of phone calls or emails made to any resident that has a history of delinquent payments to determine if there is an issue or if it's just and oversight. If you review this number, i.e. number of contacts made, and see it's low, you can make some changes that will have an impact on future sales. We call these leading indicators. You will typically be looking at a mix of leading and lagging KPIs in your dashboard. By determining the right KPIs your association board needs to look at, you can measure your performance and determine what additional actions you need to take to fulfill on your vision.

When it comes to community associations, there may be board KPIs, community KPIs, and financial KPIs. Let's take a look at each of those:

Board KPIs

How can you determine if your board is running well as a business entity? Some questions to help determine what KPIs you may want to look at include:

- **Board meetings:** Are you having regular meetings? How would you know unless your board has defined what "regular" means? For example, you could say that "Our board meets for no more than sixty minutes each month on such and such day." Once you establish frequency and set the ideal, your KPI would report how many board meetings you actually have per month so you can compare that number to your ideal.

- **Percentage of board attendees:** Want to monitor attendance rates for board meetings? Make it a KPI. You could refine your regular meeting KPI to say "The board meets once a month for no more than 60 minutes and we have 90% participation by board members." Pretty easy to measure that.

- **Punctuality:** Do your meetings start and end on time? Hopefully you are starting to get the picture on the type of things you can create and measure. Once you measure this, you can see what's actually happening and compare it to your ideal. If they don't match, you can address whatever's not working so that you start to hit your KPIs.

Other important board KPIs might be:

- Did the management report get distributed three days before the meeting?

- Did you do your elections, budgeting, planning, and reporting on time?

- Do you have a three-year plan?

- Average director tenure

- ☐ Percentage of new board members

Community KPIs

- ☐ Are people running for office? Do you have 3 to 4 people for each office?
- ☐ How many surveys did you conduct and what percentage did you get back?
- ☐ What kind of feedback did you get back?
- ☐ Do unit owners feel comfortable sharing ideas?

Financial KPIs

- ☐ Percentage of financial reports delivered on time
- ☐ Cycle time to perform periodic close
- ☐ Accuracy of financial reports
- ☐ Net income
- ☐ Percentage of delinquent payments
- ☐ Average number of tenants managed by property manager

There is a great resource called KPILibrary.com that you can reference to help brainstorm what KPIs you want to track for your association.

Five Critical Steps for Putting KPIs to Work

The next challenge is using KPI data effectively to improve decision-making. To be successful, KPI data must be measured, tracked, and rewarded. While gathering this information is not always easy, technology provides the capability to more readily compile and analyze data for each metric.

The following five steps can help you successfully implement KPI metrics and improve results.

1. **Get Buy-In**

    Involve critical individuals early when determining and selecting your company's KPIs in order to significantly increase your success. If your team was not included in this process, then they may not have the incentive or ownership to drive participation. They may not intend for the new KPI initiative to fail, but change is difficult for most of us. Bringing them into the process early on ensures their support and gives them a sense of ownership and accountability for meeting the KPIs you set.

2. **Measure**

    Almost any aspect of a business can be measured in dollars, units, percentages, or time. Even less-defined measurements like satisfaction, confidence, or perception of quality can be determined through surveying and rating. Make sure someone is assigned the responsibility for measuring these factors.

3. **Track & Distribute**

    Record and distribute the information you measure. New behaviors will fade if there is no way to share the results of the new KPIs. Further, progress in KPIs and the behaviors that support them are more likely when tracked against individual committee and board goals – not just according to activities completed. Simply monitoring activity could encourage busywork rather than smart work.

Tracking performance is strongest with an open and accessible system that everyone involved may access. If accessibility is an issue due to privacy or security of data, then frequent feedback about the status of the KPIs can be shared with those who are important to the success of the work.

4. **Incentivize Behaviors That Drive KPIs**

The most important way to drive KPI results is to reward the behaviors that produce positive results. It is human nature to be motivated by your own self-interest. However, a reward is distinct from a kickback. That's important so I am going to say it again: *a reward is distinct from a kickback*. You may need to think of creative rewards, e.g. build a reward into the management contract if they get the percentage of delinquencies down, throw a party for residents if meeting attendance is above 90% or whatever the set goal is. This applies to board members, association employees, residents, and business partners, so each of these groups must be considered when you determine how best to reward positive behaviors.

Be thoughtful about the activities you are rewarding. This may seem obvious, but many organizations are guilty of rewarding the wrong behavior. Consider that your mission is to preserve, protect, and enhance your community associations property values, but then you reward the team even when you come in under budget. Be clear on what you are rewarding and what is required to be recognized for the desired behaviors.

5. **Revisit & Revise**

Don't let too much time pass before you revisit the KPIs you've selected and ensure they are doing what you intended. Your KPIs don't need to be set in stone; you can change or improve them. You may try a few before settling on those that work best for your association.

CHAPTER SEVEN

Getting in Action: Board Strategy and Alignment

"A goal without a plan is just a wish." - Antoine de Saint-Exupery

I hope by reading up to this point, I've opened up the way you think about your board and its success, and more importantly, that you are ready to take your association board to a new level. But I'm sure you've been excited about things before and then watched them fizzle out, either because you didn't take action or you needed other people to take action and they didn't. Right? That happens all the time. Well, I am committed to making sure that doesn't happen this time. There is no secret or magic bullet to putting plans in action. You just have to do it and keep the conversation alive. How do you do that?

The first thing you have to do is write down your community association board goals and identify your association's business cycle. Everything starts from here, so even if you do this on your own at first, it's a step toward progress. Ideally, you'd get your board together and do this as a team, but even one action is better than no action at all.

We've created an Association Meeting Planner for boards that you can use to identify your goals and business cycles and to track your progress. You can download your template and as get access to other resources by visiting PBMBA.com, password: game-changer.

Your one-page plan will include your top three goals for the year and your specific business cycle so you can see it at all times. It's your dashboard. You see your business cycle, what you have to accomplish, and then you plan out your meetings for the year. The difference is instead of a "meetings as usual" approach, which typically means you are dealing with whatever needs to be dealt with right then and there in your meetings, you are now being proactive and talking about the things that sync up with your goals and business cycles. This creates meeting agendas in advance that relate back to your one-page plan with top three goals and what it's going to take to get that accomplished. You break down the goals into action items, noting *who is responsible* and *by when* so there is accountability and the overall goal gets accomplished over time. For instance, let's say one of your top three goals is to reduce delinquency in the association. You discuss what actions you need to take to reduce delinquency, perhaps:

- ☐ What is our current collection policy?
- ☐ How do we currently implement it?
- ☐ What's not working?
- ☐ Which of our strategic partners can help us with this?
- ☐ Do we use a law firm or a collections company?
- ☐ What is our percentage of delinquency now and where do we want to be?
- ☐ What is it going to take to get there?
- ☐ Are we willing to settle some of the delinquencies or come up with payment plans?

☐ How are we going to track our success each month?

It's a big, important conversation to have so a plan can be put in place, but once it is, the board can go to work and start making incremental steps each month that, over time, add up to accomplishing the goal. Yes, you may hit some roadblocks or unexpected circumstances, but you just keep dealing with it and taking actions until you work those out. Before you know it, you've got your delinquency issues solved and you can move onto new goals. You do that with each of your big goals and then go to work. This probably sounds a lot like how you've achieved other things in your life whether personal or business related, right? The difference, like we've distinguished, is most association boards don't run like a business, so these seemingly common sense approaches have been overlooked. In fact, they are unheard of in the community association world. But that doesn't have to be the case.

With these simple steps you can make a big difference in your community association and have the type of community that you are proud to give your time to and are even prouder to live in.

To access exclusive resources like our Meeting Planner, please visit PBMBA.com, password: game-changer.

www.ingramcontent.com/pod-product-compliance
Lightning Source LLC
Chambersburg PA
CBHW070333190526
45169CB00005B/1878